HONOR HE WROTE

Abhijit Naskar is the 21st century Neuroscientist and Poet who has been serving at the forefront of humankind's struggle against hate, intolerance. bigotry and fanaticism.

HONOR HE WROTE

100 Sonnets for
Humans Not Vegetables

ABHIJIT
NASKAR

Also by Abhijit Naskar

The Art of Neuroscience in Everything
Your Own Neuron: A Tour of Your Psychic Brain
The God Parasite: Revelation of Neuroscience
The Spirituality Engine
Love Sutra: The Neuroscientific Manual of Love
Homo: A Brief History of Consciousness
Neurosutra: The Abhijit Naskar Collection
Autobiography of God: Biopsy of A Cognitive Reality
Biopsy of Religions: Neuroanalysis towards Universal
Tolerance
Prescription: Treating India's Soul
What is Mind?
In Search of Divinity: Journey to The Kingdom of Conscience
Love, God & Neurons: Memoir of a scientist who found
himself by getting lost
The Islamophobic Civilization: Voyage of Acceptance
Neurons of Jesus: Mind of A Teacher, Spouse & Thinker
Neurons, Oxygen & Nanak
The Education Decree
Principia Humanitas
The Krishna Cancer
Rowdy Buddha: The First Sapiens
We Are All Black: A Treatise on Racism
The Bengal Tigress: A Treatise on Gender Equality
Either Civilized or Phobic: A Treatise on Homosexuality
Wise Mating: A Treatise on Monogamy
Illusion of Religion: A Treatise on Religious
Fundamentalism
The Film Testament
Human Making is Our Mission: A Treatise on Parenting
I Am The Thread: My Mission
7 Billion Gods: Humans Above All
Lord is My Sheep: Gospel of Human
Morality Absolute
A Push in Perception
Let The Poor Be Your God
Conscience over Nonsense
Saint of The Sapiens
Time to Save Medicine

Fabric of Humanity
Build Bridges not Walls: In the name of Americana
The Constitution of The United Peoples of Earth
Lives to Serve Before I Sleep
When Humans Unite: Making A World Without Borders
All For Acceptance
Monk Meets World
Mission Reality
Citizens of Peace: Beyond The Savagery of Sovereignty
Operation Justice: To Make A Society That Needs No Law
See No Gender
The Gospel of Technology
Every Generation Needs Caretakers: The Gospel of
Patriotism
Aşkanjali: The Sufi Sermon
Mad About Humans: World Maker's Almanac
Revolution Indomable
When Call The People: My World My Responsibility
No Foreigner Only Family
Hurricane Humans: Give me accountability, I'll give you
peace
Ain't Enough to Look Human
Servitude is Sanctitude
Time To End Democracy: The Meritocratic Manifesto
I Vicdansaadet Speaking: No Rest Till The World is Lifted
Boldly Comes Justice: Sentient not Silent
Good Scientist: When Science and Service Combine
Sleepless for Society
Neden Türk: The Gospel of Secularism
Martyr Meets World: To Solve The Hard Problem of
Inhumanity
The Shape of A Human: Our America Their America
When Veins Ignite: Either Integration or Degradation
Heart Force One: Need No Gun to Defend Society
Solo Standing on Guard: Life Before Law
Generation Corazon: Nationalism is Terrorism
Mucize Insan: When The World is Family
Hometown Human: To Live For Soil and Society
Girl Over God: The Novel (Abi Naskar Adventures Book 1)
Gente Mente Adelante: Prejudice Conquered is World
Conquered
Earthquakin' Egalitarian: I Die Everyday So Your Children
Can Live
Giants in Jeans: 100 Sonnets of United Earth

Vatican Virus: The Forbidden Fiction (Abi Naskar
Adventures Book 2)
Karadeniz Chronicle: The Novel (Abi Naskar Adventures
Book 3)
Şehit Sevda Society: Even in Death I Shall Live
Handcrafted Humanity: 100 Sonnets For A Blunderful
World
Mücadele Muhabbet: Gospel of An Unarmed Soldier
Making Britain Civilized: How to Gain Readmission to The
Human Race
Dervish Advaitam: Gospel of Sacred Feminines and Holy
Fathers

DEDICATION

To all the unsung poets of the world.

CONTENTS

1. **Honor He Wrote (Sonnet 1)**

ABHIJIT NASKAR

Sonnet 1

Honor He Wrote
(The Sonnet)

I am not a writer, writers have limits,
I have none, I only have responsibility,
The responsibility to unite the world,
The responsibility to humanize humanity.
We are setting out on this journey,
With the awareness of being responsible,
For responsibility makes one honorable,
Honor makes one responsible.
Fervor of honor is beginning to fade,
From the fabric of society and self.
It is definitely no sign of progress,
In fact it is a sign of utter decadence.
Honor is, in truth, another name for character.
With the demise of honor all good will disappear.

2. Conviction & Duty
(Sonnet 2 - 4)

Sonnet 2

If the idea of honor were to disappear,
Upon becoming intrinsic to human nature,
That would have been a different story,
A story worth a thousand celebration.
The fact of the matter is quite the opposite,
Honor is fading for materialism is taking over,
And if we let this continue for much longer,
Values and virtues will be hard to even remember.
So let's take stock of the bone of our back,
Without which civilization will fall into pieces.
We've spent long enough in pursuit of luxury,
It's time to live bravely on purpose, not as leeches.
Enough with climbing the greasy pole of validation!
Grab hold of your backbone, toughen up your conviction.

Sonnet 3

No conviction ought to be final except assimilation.
No belief ought to be ultimate except collectivity.
No tradition ought to be eternal except compassion.
No habit ought to be incorrigible except humility.
No assumption should dictate action over awareness.
No opinion should rule perception over reason.
No intellect should be given life's reins over warmth.
No edict should define lifestyle over unification.
Human life remains human as long as we are growing.
Cessation of growth is cessation of civilized existence.
Stagnated mind is the root of all hate, war and disorder.
Mind, never rigid, is the source of sense and sapience.
One dreamer awake in love invigorates the whole world.
Soldiers of love live alone, rest just sleep, howl and crawl.

Sonnet 4

Raise your power in silence,
Become a dynamite of resilience.
Head high and chest emboldened,
March on with uncorrupt conscience.
Be the heart that loves and lifts,
Be the hand that shares might.
Feel the talk and talk the feel,
Be the mirror of sight beyond sight.
Be the first when no one comes,
Be the last when all are gone.
Be the one who sits not still,
Be the rays of a dutiful dawn.
You are the order you seek outside.
To be human is to put coldness aside.

3. God, Silence & Miracle
(Sonnet 5 - 7)

Sonnet 5

The God Sonnet

I gave you the tablets at Sinai,
I drove your chariot at Kurukshetra.
I gave you the ayats word by word,
I woke up Siddhartha 'n the carpenter.
No matter the time, age 'n technology,
I always rise to treat the common cold.
Amidst a world full of sore coldness,
I only need ten vessels absurdly bold.
I have nothing to do with perfection,
Far from it, I've got plenty to improve.
With each new vessel my sight broadens,
With each identity my existence renewed.
Keeper am I of this terrestrial neighborhood.
I am your innermost fire of god and good.

Sonnet 6

Sonnet of Silence

I am the loudest when I am silent,
My lips are shut yet I speak treasures.
Speech without heart is nothing but noise,
Listen to my silence, you'll hear the universe.
Words spoken with mere lips reach nowhere,
For it's the heart that makes words alive.
Tell people who you are without saying a word,
Speak from your very core, they'll listen alright.
I repeat, silent people have the loudest hearts,
For when you speak less you get to listen more.
The more you listen the more you are heard,
The more you hear the more you get to grow.
Set the words on fire, let them all turn to ashes.
Tell people who you are without all the speeches.

Sonnet 7

Care not whether you see change,
Care only to be the needed change.
Care not about the fruits of action,
Care only to walk the human lane.
Walking on water without drowning,
Is not miracle, but an illusive trade.
Real miracle is walking on earth,
Without drowning in hate.
In the absence of accountability,
Be the only shining example.
In the absence of love and humility,
Be a loving and living fable.
Whining about all the evil is of no use.
One dream, one mission - oneness absolute.

16

4. The Case of Life (Sonnet 8 - 10)

Sonnet 8

Give me a spark of your nerves,
I'll turn it into thunder strike.
Give me a tremor of your lips,
I'll turn it into landslide.
Give me a teardrop of your eyes,
I'll turn it into tsunami.
Give me the sweat of your labor,
I'll turn it into hydroelectricity.
Give me a beat of your heart,
I'll turn it into an earthquake.
Give me a touch of your fingers,
I'll turn it into society's duct tape.
Ingredients of reform are born of your veins.
Renounce your apathy and reform will rain.

Sonnet 9

The case of life is a case of kindness,
The case of reform is a case of unself.
The case of growth is a case of correction,
The case of joy is a case beyond the self.
To unself the soul is to unfold happiness,
To disavow destiny is to write destiny.
To bring down the walls is to build bridges,
To refute inhumanity is to practice humanity.
Upon our indifference jungle sustains,
Upon our accountability worlds unfold.
Requirement of civilization is plain 'n simple,
Appearance is nothing if hands don't unfold.
You know why we have two hands 'n one mouth,
So that we may stop arguing 'n help each other out.

Sonnet 10

Do you hear your heart beating,
Then at times do you worry in vain!
Do you fall flat on your face sometimes,
Then at your own will you rise again!
Do you find yourself talking to yourself,
Then at times do you laugh at yourself!
Do you wanna bite someone's head off,
Then when needed reach out to help!
Do you ever think, 'what do I think about',
Then at times do you feel sure of everything!
Do you ever fight spiders in your dreams,
Then at times stand boldly against all haunting!
All this is no disease but mere human condition.
Human is one who gives not in to the inner demon.

5. Why The Candle Burns
(Sonnet 11 - 13)

Sonnet 11

You wanna get laid?
Get laid, but with consent.
You wanna jump off a cliff?
Just jump, with an active brain.
You wanna try booze?
Try it, but with moderation.
You wanna smoke weed?
Do it, but with self-regulation.
Try out everything you wanna try,
Figure out right 'n wrong for yourself.
It is your life, test it to its limits, but,
Be sure not to harm others in the process.
Get it all over with, for plenty work remains.
Live to build a world, not to pamper shallow tenets.

Sonnet 12

After all this time, the sun doesn't say to us,
Listen you guys, you owe all your light to me.
The trees do not grab us by the throat,
And yell, all your air and food are my charity.
A candle does not burn to be appraised,
But because to burn is the purpose of a candle.
A candle not burning is no candle at all,
Be a burning candle and live life purpose-driven.
Life is a vessel of infinite majesty and potential,
Let us not let it rot at the shore playing safe.
Come hail or high water, let us be shredded,
Let us be annihilated in service and in help.
Let us be human, let us be alive across all narrowness.
Let us be the shining beacon of supreme unselfishness.

Sonnet 13

Love Logic Intention
(The Drunken Sonnet)

Love that keeps you sober is no love,
There is no soldier only drunken lover.
A thousand dazzling Vegas turn bleak,
When the soul shines with love's labor.
For once, let go of all judgment my friend,
Wipe out all cynicism from your core.
Close your eyes and look with your heart,
Either we are lovers or at death's door.
Nutty logic makes nice machines,
Nutty love makes a good society.
Scars of love add definition to life,
Tears of a lover are diamonds of divinity.
Right world is the result of right intention.
If you want light, burn, burn 'n burn again.

Sonnet 13 - Turkish

Aşk Mantık İnsanlık
(Sarhoş Şiir)

Mantıksal aşk aşk değildir,
Sarhoş aşıktan başka asker yok.
İnsan aşk için çılgın olmazsa,
Cennet gibi hayat bile hayat yok.
Bir kez, tüm aklını feda et dostum,
Bir kez, tüm mantığı unut.
Gözlerini kapat, kalbinle bak,
Ya biz seviyoruz, ya da ölüyoruz.
Aşkın gözyaşlarında ilahi bir derya var,
Gözyaşlarınla egonu iyice yıka.
Bir aşıkin kalp atışı insanlığın müziğidir,
Sevgiliyiz biz, bizim ailemiz bütün dünya.
Doğru dünya doğru niyetin sonucudur.
Işık istiyorsan, güneş gibi yan - hadi beyler!

6. Life, Strife & Crime
    (Sonnet 14 - 16)

Sonnet 14

Today
(The Sonnet)

Today, we ain't no partisan poophead.
Today, we are just plain human.
Today, we ain't no intellectual ding-dong.
Today, we are just plain human.
Today, we ain't no ideological blockhead.
Today, we are just plain human.
Today, we ain't no religious hard case.
Today, we are just plain human.
Today, we ain't slaves to class 'n luxury.
Today, we are just plain human.
Today, we ain't no vermin after self-care.
Today, we are just plain human.
I know very well, that day is not today.
So, let us start the work right this very day.

Sonnet 14 - Spanish

Hoy
(El Soneto)

Hoy, no somos religiosos.
Hoy, solo somos humanos.
Hoy, no somos politicos.
Hoy, solo somos humanos.
Hoy, no somos intelectuales.
Hoy, solo somos humanos.
Hoy, no somos lógicos.
Hoy, solo somos humanos.
Hoy, no somos sofisticados.
Hoy, solo somos humanos.
Hoy, no somos ricos o pobres.
Hoy, solo somos humanos.
Sé bien que ese día no es hoy.
¡Vamos, comencemos el cambio hoy!

Sonnet 14 - Turkish

Bugün

(Bir Hayat Şiiri)

Bugün, biz dindar değiliz.
Bugün, biz sadece insanız.
Bugün, bütün siyaseti unuttuk.
Çünkü bugün, biz sadece insanız.
Bugün, biz entelektüel değiliz.
Çünkü bugün, biz insan olduk.
Bugün, beynimizde mantık yoktur.
Çünkü bugün, biz insan olduk.
Bugün, lükse hiç ihtiyacımız yok.
Çünkü bugün, biz insan olduk.
Bugün, sadelik en büyük zenginliktir.
Çünkü bugün, gerçekten insan olduk.
İyi biliyorum, o gün bugün değil.
Yolculuğa bugün başlayalım, yarın değil.

Sonnet 15

34

It is no time for comfort,
It is no time for leisure.
Plenty lives are to be lifted,
Beyond all personal pleasure.
All are lost in glamor 'n glory,
All are lost in gratification.
All care about me, me 'n me,
All live for self-preservation.
You for one, live for others,
Be the hand that wipes tears.
Be the one that reaches out,
Across all selfish fears.
Always say, I am love, I am life,
I am the answer to all human strife.

Sonnet 16

Antidote to Crime
(The Sonnet)

The way to a crime-free world is simple,
But it lies outside of all the legal 'n partisan muck.
Take away the guns from the kids on the street,
Put books in their hands and food in their stomach.
By the time they grow up into young adults,
The prehistoric warmongers will be in death bed.
The children whose childhood you restored,
Will all be ready to hold the reins of world stage.
Law, policy 'n all that stuff surely have their place,
But not as the antidote to crime, chaos 'n descension.
The permanent antidote to crime is education alone,
Law 'n policy are just to ensure its true democratization.
More than trying a crime, focus on treating environment.
Feed the hungry 'n establish education, free from any debt.

7. Correction & Crisis
(Sonnet 17 - 19)

Sonnet 17

Can we create a world without crime?
Can we create a world without injustice?
Can we create a world without tyranny?
Can we create a world without malice?
Can we create a world without prejudice?
Can we create a world without hatefulness?
Can we create a world without assumption?
Can we create a world without differences?
Can we create a world without bigotry?
Can we create a world without dollarism?
Can we create a world without coldness?
Can we create a world without divisionism?
Only in fairytales exists a world of perfection.
Our mission is not utopia, but eternal correction.

Sonnet 18

What's there to correct, I'm sheer perfection,
Some egotistical snobs continue to ponder.
That right there is what we need to correct,
Our unwillingness to acknowledge our error.
To make mistakes is very much human,
But refusing to acknowledge them is animal.
Once acknowledged then we can correct them,
In willful self-correction we become noble.
Be a rebel all you want, but be wise as well,
Enough to recognize when you've made a mess.
Be sure of your conviction all you want,
But make sure it doesn't impair improvement.
There is no knowledge, only lesser ignorance.
There is no absolute truth, only lesser falseness.

Sonnet 19

From error to error, we'll correct our errors.
From failure to failure, we shall rise high.
From despair to despair, our fears disappear.
From scar to scar, our heart learns to fly.
From one jinx to another, we become destiny.
From darkness to darkness, we become light.
One wound to another, we become the cure.
From one loss to another, we understand life.
Dust bite after dust bite, all dust become ointment.
One lost road after another, we draw a new map.
Teardrops upon teardrops, all tears turn elixir.
One screw-up after another, we learn to grow up.
One heartbreak to another, we become the healer.
Bearing crisis upon crisis, we shall rise as creator.

8.   Heartbreak & Braveheart
     (Sonnet 20 - 22)

Sonnet 20

The more you break me, the stronger I become.
The more you hate me, the gentler I become.
The more you mock me, the kinder I become.
The more you alienate me, the braver I become.
The more you betray me, the more I learn to trust.
The more you disappoint me, the more I feel electrified.
The more you take advantage, the more I learn to care.
The more you backstab me, the more I am energized.
The more you humiliate me, the more I gain humility.
The more you laugh at me, the more I learn to smile.
More you kick me around, more my spine is straightened.
The more you drag me down, the higher I end up flying.
Every bad behavior directed at me amplifies my power.
The broken humans of the world make the greatest healer.

Sonnet 21

If you are afraid to be broken, you'll never be whole.
If you are afraid to be lost, you'll never find the path.
If you are afraid to be hurt, you are already crippled.
If you are afraid that you'll lose, you have already lost.
Maps are made by those who aren't afraid to be lost.
Because of them rest of humanity can relish new roads.
Few bravehearts must always be sleepless for society.
Nobody could sleep in peace if it weren't for them heroes.
There may always be some fear as well as insecurities.
That is not the problem, for it is healthy human condition.
What's unhealthy is to leave the reins of your life to them.
Awake, arise o braveheart, and do away with stagnation.
Life without failures and heartbreaks ain't no life at all.
Fail a little, lose a little, but live to the fullest, quirks 'n all.

Sonnet 22

You don't know love, till you've known heartbreak,
You won't know sight, till you've known blindness.
You don't know courage, till you've felt helpless,
You won't know light, till you've been in darkness.
Darkest clouds herald the brightest sunshine,
Direst circumstances make the bravest of character.
Heavier the rainfall, more breathtaking the rainbow,
Steeper the hill to climb, sweeter the summit vista.
Once your back is against the wall, only way is through,
You won't know integrity, till you are left in pieces.
Lose all identity, only then you'll know to be human,
You won't know wholeness, till you've felt nothingness.
More ominous the night, more spectacular the daybreak.
Till we're wiped out for a purpose, there's no upliftment.

9. Gender & Clothes
(Sonnet 23 - 25)

50

Sonnet 23

My life is your life, your struggle is my struggle,
Thus speaks the being who knows existence.
Existence is existence when we exist for others,
Life rooted in selfishness is but a life of a rodent.
Injustice on a single soul is violation of my own rights,
Thus speaks the one who knows accountability.
The injustice that you foolishly choose to ignore,
Soon will come back to haunt your progeny.
I am safe and sound, who cares about the world,
Such attitude does not suit a living human.
To care for one's own family is nothing special,
To also care for the neighbor's family is truly human.
Gender, faith, color, clothes, nothing must be a rigid sanctum.
A mind united is a world united, this is my only dictum.

Sonnet 24

The Gender Sonnet

Woman means not weakling, but wonder.
Woman means not obstinate, but original.
Woman means not man-slave, but mother.
Woman means not amorous, but amiable.
Woman means not neurotic, but nimble.
Man mustn't mean medieval, but moral.
Man mustn't mean abusive, but affable.
Man mustn't mean nefarious, but noble.
Trans doesn't mean titillating, but tenacious.
Trans doesn't mean riff-raff, but radiant.
It doesn't mean abhorrent, but affectionate.
It ain't nasty and sick, but nerved and sentient.
Gender has no role in society except in bed.
Person is known by character, not dongs 'n peaches.

Sonnet 25

Freedom of Dress
(The Sonnet)

Freedom of dress is as important,
As freedom of press, that's common sense.
If we're still stuck with squabbles on clothes,
When will we manifest character's radiance!
What does it matter, what we wear,
As long as we walk with our head held high!
Anything that strengthens our backbone,
Is worth the fight of a thousand lifetime.
Clothes perish, so does the body in them,
But a well-built character keeps on shining.
Focus on conduct across all shallow exterior,
Let burning dogs burn, you just keep dazzling.
I repeat, heed not the honks of primeval puritans.
Own your booty and trample all condemnation.

10. Short Sight & Abnormality
(Sonnet 26 - 28)

Sonnet 26

Sonnet of Short Dress

There is no short dress, only short sight,
No obscene outfit, only eyes of obscenity.
The world is no man's family heirloom,
That it should be cherished by the men only.
Instead of restricting a girl's right to expression,
Teach boys, short dress isn't a sign of consent.
If women cannot walk around freely as men do,
Better sentence all men to lifetime imprisonment.
Let all girls hear it loud, wear what you like to wear,
Walk around naked if that's what you really want.
And when an animal makes unwanted advances,
Activate your knee 'n crush their beloved balls to pulp.
Girls don't need protecting, they ain't fragile showpiece.
Let's just raise boys as decent humans, not entitled bullies.

Sonnet 27

In a world full of bullies, being gentle is abnormal.
In a world full of arrogance, humility is abnormal.
In a world full of dollarism, charity is abnormal.
In a world full of cockiness, conscience is abnormal.
In a world full of compromise, integrity is abnormal.
In a world full of apathy, empathy is abnormal.
In a world of indifference, accountability is abnormal.
In a world full of assumption, warmth is abnormal.
In a world full of prejudice, reasoning is abnormal.
In a world full of conspiracy, science is abnormal.
In a world full of bigotry, assimilation is abnormal.
In a world full of influencing, expertise is abnormal.
So what do we do, where do we start to change all this!
How about the thought, that we really wanna change this!

Sonnet 28

It's one thing to be a feminist, another to be hysteric.
It's one thing to be religious, another to be obsolete.
It's one thing to be an atheist, another to be a moron.
One thing to be a climate activist, another to be a lunatic.
It's one thing to have intellect, another to be an egotist.
It's one thing to have free speech, another to speak hate.
It's one thing to study science, another to be a smart nitwit.
One thing to study philosophy, another to be a dunderhead.
It's one thing to be a preacher, another to be salesperson.
It's one thing to be crazy in love, another to be control freak.
One thing to be public servant, another to be public parent.
One thing to be reformist, another to be a short-fused terrorist.
The greatest of convictions often gets corrupted by egotism.
So every now and then expose yourself to some gentefication.*

*gente means people, hence, by gentefication,
I refer to humanification or humanizing

11. Cavebound No More
(Sonnet 29 - 31)

Sonnet 29

Before you beautify, learn to gentefy.
Before you modernize, learn to gentefy.
Before you scientify, learn to gentefy.
Before you philosophize, learn to gentefy.
Before you justify, learn to gentefy.
Before you dogmatize, learn to gentefy.
Before you smartify, learn to gentefy.
Before you glamorize, learn to gentefy.
Before you class-ify, learn to gentefy.
Before you culturize, learn to gentefy.
Before you mummify, learn to gentefy.
Before you analyze, learn to gentefy.
Tu gente es mi gente*, thus we're civilized.
To be gentefied is to be sanctified.

*Your people are my people.

Sonnet 30

64

In people is my liberty,
In people is my joy.
In people is my sanity,
To be sacrificed is my ploy.
People are my salvation,
People are my aspiration.
People are my ambition,
People are my absolution.
My deities are the destitute,
To make them equal is my promise.
My church is at the feet of the helpless,
To lift them up is my worship.
The aim is to elevate the alienated,
Not submit to the snobs and savages.

Sonnet 31

To think outside the circle of self,
Is the original act of a human being.
To think outside personal benefit,
Is the beginning of civilized living.
Move from individuality to community,
And lo, your light makes animality disappear.
Move from security to self-sacrifice,
And lo, a nightcrawler turns into humanizer.
It's good to love your family as the world,
Even greater is to love the world as your family.
Till separation between family and world withers,
You won't know the full expanse of your humanity.
Wipe out all prehistoric circles that keep you cavebound.
Enough with this cave life, it's time to be unbound!

12. The Gentalist (Sonnet 32 - 34)

Sonnet 32

Don't wait up for destiny to happen to you,
Stand up and be the destiny of the world.
I didn't wait for the world to happen to me,
I stood up and happened to the world.
Sit no more holding out for a magical messiah,
All the world's magic is just human creation.
Magic is just code for human determination,
There is nothing paranormal, only dedication.
No more bowing in front of the altar of tradition,
Be a radical star and explode for your purpose.
Your light shall live on in people's memory,
As you pour out all life for the good of others.
Destiny and fate are constructs of fear and insecurity.
Conquer your fears and rise as the human almighty.

Sonnet 33

There is no lord almighty, only human almighty,
No magic and mysticism, only nature and oneness.
There are no ten commandments, only one,
Compassion has no religion, character has no race.
There's no law above life, life alone is the supreme law,
And stagnant law does more harm than action illegal.
There is no holy trinity, only humanity up on its toes,
It is always the human mind playing the triangle.
No more dogmas, no more doctrines and manifestos,
Let us be forthright 'n just foster the spirit of affection.
Once we learn to celebrate each other's existence,
There won't be any need for artificial occasion.
Awake, arise o dynamite, blow up all old paradigm.
Don't fight it, or cuss it, just overwhelm it with your lifeline.

Sonnet 34

The Gentalist Sonnet

I only ask one thing of my soldier – everything!
Give up all, so that those with nothing receive life.
What can I give to thee, except for this life of mine,
Says the brave gentalist across all personal strife.
Gente means people, and people are the music of life.
Love the people, lift the people, people are the way.
Not your people, not my people, it's all one people.
Once you feel it in your bones, uplift is on its way.
I don't believe in a messiah, I don't believe in a god,
'Cause I'm far too accountable for my society, my world.
Thus speaks the gentalist, burning with a sense of duty,
Thus speaks the living aid, who ain't no mythical lord.
If a chunk of alum can purify a bucket of putrid water,
Your heart can purify the world with its gentalist power.

13. When Love Enters (Sonnet 35 - 37)

Sonnet 35

Power is only power, if it helps the people,
Heart is only heart, if it lifts other hearts.
Sight is only sight, if it eases suffering,
Life is only life, if it's lived for others.
To breathe is no sign of life,
The real sign of life is kindness.
Respiration is the work of lungs,
Whereas life is the work of humanness.
Seed of life is not joy but unselfishness,
It's through unselfishness that uplift comes.
But being unselfish doesn't mean without self,
It means to expand 'n contain the whole universe.
Oneness is the sum total of all eternal truth.
If it doesn't lead to oneness, it's anything but truth.

Sonnet 36

There is no truth, only lesser falsity,
There is no knowledge, only lesser ignorance.
Make not knowledge your ultimate purpose,
Use knowledge to expand your heart's radiance.
Real knowledge always leads to expansion,
If it does not, it is just another delusion.
Knowledge that helps you alone and not others,
Is but an endeavor of a concrete barbarian.
Your knowledge of a thousand books is nothing,
If it doesn't stir inside you the fire of humanizing.
If it does nothing to elevate human condition,
Better blow all facts and figures to smithereens.
Knowledge without humanity is intellectual stupidity.
Better be dope and kind, than a cold carcass of logicality.

Sonnet 37

When love enters the heart,
Reason flees the head.
When duty enters the heart,
Apathy flees the head.
When acceptance enters the heart,
Judgment flees the head.
When humanity enters the heart,
Sectarianism flees the head.
But none of it really enters,
From outside into your veins.
Just like the stains of society,
All detergent is born in your brain.
We are the answer to all our devastation.
We are the revolution to our own delusion.

14. Language & Learning
(Sonnet 38 - 40)

Sonnet 38

It is all merely an illusion,
Let's make it a humane one.
Patriotism boils in our blood,
But for the wrong reason.
Patriotism of our ancestors,
Won't do any good to our world.
We are new humans of a new world,
Let's rewrite patriotism 'n make it evolved.
Be the torch of civilized patriotism,
And dive heart 'n soul for universality.
Be a shimmering star of selflessness,
Let your veins overflow with amity.
Humanize your veins, nerves, blood 'n bones.
Be the fountainhead you are, 'n let expansion pour.

Sonnet 39

82

The more I write the more I realize,
The inane limitations of language.
Never be a stickler for terminology,
It only impedes your humanness.
If anything, try to set humanity free,
From the bounds of words 'n speech.
Let the world know who you are,
But without being a linguistic leech.
Behavior alone defines a person,
Make behavior your background.
Neither culture, nor geography,
It's only in action that identity is found.
Unfold your today beyond your yesterday,
Or else, there'll be no tomorrow, only decay.

Sonnet 40

To learn from yesterday is growth,
To be stuck in yesterday is decay.
To look for a better future is vision,
To be stuck there only causes dismay.
Glance at the past, aim for the future,
But keep your feet grounded in present.
Learn from history, envision the destiny,
'N dive in today with your sweat valiant.
Memory is meant to give you ground,
Not to impede in your prosperity.
Vision is to embolden your footsteps,
Not to disconnect you from reality.
Some make history their prison, some future.
Bid goodbye to those inmates, 'n be a timemaster.

15. Past, Present & Time-building
(Sonnet 41 - 43)

Sonnet 41

Don't worship your past,
At the expense of your present.
Don't glorify the future,
At the expense of the present.
Don't worship the dead,
At the expense of the living.
Don't admire the unborn,
While overlooking the living.
It's only by lifting the living that,
We build a better world for all progeny.
It's only by being kind to the living,
That we truly honor our ancestry.
Honor is earned not begged for.
Honor the living, 'n all time will be grateful.

Sonnet 42

Either you build time,
Or you are buried in time.
Either you share life with others,
Or selfishness spoils your lifeline.
Either you foster your own ideas,
Or you are buried in dead ideologies.
Either you build your own reality,
Or you are buried in society's insecurity.
Either you nourish your humanity,
Or you are buried in inhumanity.
Step out of the brothel of bigotry,
Or stay forever buried in tribal tendency.
The world doesn't become better by brooding.
Don't like what you see - then start working.

Sonnet 43

You asked, do I have just one outfit?
I say, simplicity is the outfit of a reformer.
You asked, why don't I take a vacation?
I say, vacation is luxury for a reformer.
You asked, what do I do for fun?
I say, I renounced fun so you may thrive.
You said, I shouldn't take life so seriously.
I say, you 'n I have different definitions of life.
To most people life may be about having fun,
I only know one life, the kind that lifts the society.
People may pursue pleasure all they want,
My single pursuit is that of universal amity.
Instead of questioning my humanitarian insanity,
Ask yourself, what exactly would you call sanity!

16. There's No Social Work
(Sonnet 44 - 46)

Sonnet 44

What you call sanity, I call selfishness.
What you call practicality, I call selfishness.
What you call sensibility, I call selfishness.
What you call fortune, I call selfishness.
What you call economy, I call selfishness.
What you call progress, I call selfishness.
What you call intelligence, I call selfishness.
What you call success, I call selfishness.
What you call nationality, I call selfishness.
What you call culture, I call selfishness.
What you call heritage, I call selfishness.
What you call tradition, I call selfishness.
To be selfish is to be the walking dead.
To be dead to selfishness is a life well led.

Sonnet 45

There's no social work, only family work,
There's no social uplift, only family uplift.
There's no social issue, only family issue,
There's no social service, only self-service.
There's no social reform, only life's reform,
There's no social science, only mental science.
There's no collectivism, only self-realization,
There's no sociology, only common sense.
There's no political science, only life science,
No international relations, only human relations.
There's no diplomacy, only communication,
There is no geopolitics, only amalgamation.
There is no foreigner or stranger, only family,
No social responsibility, only family responsibility.

Sonnet 46

What is society - a reflection of the self.
What is community - proof of togetherness.
What is neighborhood - a promise of care.
What is civilization - a pledge of hatelessness.
What are the alleys - playground of innocence.
What are the streets - bearer of ascension.
What is the soil - a reminder of humility.
What is the sky - a reminder for expansion.
What are the rivers - epitome of perseverance.
What are the mountains - proof of zealousness.
What is the cactus - proof of unsubmission.
What is the mountain goat - proof of resilience.
What is the universe - manifestation of our will.
Humanize that will, 'n all troubles will turn nil.

17. Unsubmission & Unblocking
(Sonnet 47 - 49)

Sonnet 47

Be the cactus, a proof of unsubmission,
And blossom amidst the fiercest environment.
In a world primed with the probability of hate,
Be love impossible and lift all lost in lament.
Aspire to expire for a cause uncausable,
And your heart will shine with light untamable.
When all go berserk for sect as bozos on booze,
Be the sectless sapiens and stand indivisible.
When all are possessed with the libido of liberty,
Be the first one standing, responsible 'n righteous.
In a world founded on unfounded assumptions,
Be the first ink of understanding unpresumptuous.
Blockheads and blockhearts have only blocked amity.
It's time to unblock, unfold and undivide our psyche.

Sonnet 48

We need to unblock our head alright,
More than that we need to unblock our heart.
We need to foster some reason alright,
More than that we gotta make love unbarred.
Problem is, when the head opens, heart is shut,
Without warmth of the heart, head is just a bone.
Without the intervention of reason from the head,
Heart is just another brutish muscle most unhoned.
Often I use heart as synonym for humanity,
Though technically it's a symposium of good 'n bad.
That's why even the heart needs to be humanized,
For our infinite potential for good to engulf all bad.
It is no longer about choosing between heart 'n head,
It's about living 'n behaving as a whole human undivided.

Sonnet 49

When you've written as much as I have, it's impossible,
Not to have seemingly contradictory statements.
They seem so 'cause you only look at words, not context,
Context constitutes 90% of a message, words only 10%.
This is what I've been referring to as limitation of language,
Be not sure of words, until you've asked without judgment.
As I have said repeatedly, never stick too rigidly to words,
Take a step beyond the words and realize the message.
Nature gave us language to be bridge among beings,
But we turned it into yet another tool of self-aggrandizing,
Like we have done with the faculty of reason 'n intellect,
Like we have done with all our religious dogmatizing.
Enough I say, with the meaningless pursuit of self-glorification!
Enough with this craving for bickering as pests of putrefaction!

18. Difference & Discrimination
(Sonnet 50 - 52)

Sonnet 50

The problem is not our differences,
It is that we are fragile creatures.
The slightest spark of disagreement,
Makes us find an enemy in others.
Imagine if we agreed on everything,
How boring this world would be!
So let's bite each other's head off,
Let's disagree most enthusiastically.
No difference can tear us apart,
Till we compromise our humanity.
It is okay to disagree with each other,
But not to hate the other 'cause we disagree.
Differences are not a failure of humanity,
Differences are a test of our humanity.

Sonnet 51

Difference & Discrimination
(The Sonnet)

There ain't no difference that can't be conquered,
Except for those that are rooted in inhumanity.
A bigot's emphasis on their supremacy over others,
Is not a difference in opinion but clinical insanity.
Nobody is inferior to nobody in this world of ours,
Except for those who think of others as such.
Neither ancestry nor luxury defines a character,
Conduct alone defines character, above all fuss.
Say, discrimination is not a difference in opinion,
It's an act that sets animals apart from humans.
Free speech is a phenomenon of human society,
Hate speech is an act of stoneage barbarians.
Let us distinguish differences from discrimination,
Then celebrate differences while treating discrimination.

Sonnet 52

Inclusion over exclusion,
Celebration over segregation,
Diversity over homogeneity,
Assimilation over discrimination,
Self-sacrifice over domination,
Heartification over indoctrination,
Conversation over condemnation,
Camaraderie over condescension,
Music of amity over scream of vanity,
Colors of comity over kool-aid of cruelty,
Jingle of jesting over gestating a jungle,
Whispers of wonder over whining apathy,
Thus we'll make a dent on destiny's design,
For we are the designer as well as the design.

19. Muster The Motive
(Sonnet 53 - 55)

Sonnet 53

Better a marvelheaded idiot,
Than a marbleheaded bigot.
Better a self-proclaimed dope,
Than an arrogant dilettante.
Better a kindhearted commoner,
Than a cockeyed intellectualist.
Better an egalitarian infidel,
Than a dogmatizing evangelist.
All dogmas are born in the mind,
So is the duster to wipe them.
It is up to you what will you be,
Vessel of dogma or the duster untamed!
Convert none, help all, without imposition.
Let uplift be the motive behind all conviction.

Sonnet 54

Motive makes the mind,
Motive makes the world.
What is your real motive,
And is it enough bold?
Intention is the seed of change,
But the interesting part is something else.
In the absence of an intention for good,
Greed and corruption keep making mess.
Darkness is natural, where light is not,
Prejudice is strong, where love is bleak.
If nobody else, be love and light yourself,
Be the new chapter upon nature's fabric.
Muster the motive for a magnificent mundo.
Your motive will charge your feet beyond all woe.

Sonnet 55

Where you need to blow your top,
You keep quiet and walk away.
Where you need to keep quiet,
You blow your top like you're unswayed.
Distinguish triviality from tyranny,
Inconvenience from injustice.
Walk away from petty squabbles, but,
Stand up to oppression without cowardice.
Justice begins with a just civilian, not a politician,
Order begins with an orderly commoner, not a copper.
So the question is, are you a just 'n orderly commoner,
Or just more slime that leaves all to the warmongers?
The government's job is not to govern but listen,
And the citizens' duty is to speak as beings nonpartisan.

20. Dreamwalking & Hatebusting
(Sonnet 56 - 58)

Sonnet 56

It's the citizens' duty to make a nation nonpartisan,
Government is meant to serve as powerless figurehead.
All my hopes lie in the hands of accountable citizens,
A good politician acts a citizen, not political dunderhead.
So no more procrastination with the curation of society,
No more playing hooky in the school of life and sanity.
Be the politician that you seek in the sewers of state,
Not by law but by an indefatigable accountability.
Democracy means rule of the people, not sleep of people,
Yet that's what it means to people 'n politicians alike.
But shhh, nobody is supposed to admit any of it in public,
For discretion is the better part of a society of sleeping mice.
Let sleeping slime sleep, if you are human, take charge now.
Dream with your eyes open and keep your democracy vow.

Sonnet 57

Dreams that we witness in sleep, ain't no dream,
Real dream is the one that doesn't let us sleep.
Only when mindful martyrs work without blink,
Rest of the world has a peaceful sleep.
I have been sleepless ever since I came of age,
Such is the madness of the dream of assimilation.
The thought of rest rarely enters my mind,
No matter how much the climb causes desolation.
No dream comes to fruition without restless nights,
No sun ever rises without first crossing darkness.
No mortal ever turns immortal without self-sacrifice,
No world is ever beautified without martyr's madness.
Enough with the snobbish nonsense of dream analyzing!
All know sleepwalking, now let 'em witness dreamwalking!

Sonnet 58

In a world full of sleepwalkers,
What's needed is a dreamwalker.
In a world full of vacationers,
What's needed is an invigorizer.
In a society full of world travelers,
What's needed is a mind traveler.
In a universe full of space explorers,
What's needed is a heart explorer.
In a neighborhood full of naysayers,
What's needed is an energizer.
In this hellhole of hatelusters,
What's needed is a hatebuster.
It takes nothing to sustain a cruel jungle.
To build society it takes love unbreakable.

21. Tale of A Lover Divine
(Sonnet 59 - 61)

Sonnet 59

World is My Valentine
(The Sonnet)

My first and foremost love is society,
Romance 'n things are second priority.
My love seeks not to be loved in return,
In fact, my love thrives in cold nonreciprocity.
Mine is not to reason why, mine is to love and die,
There's no greater love than that of a one-sided lover.
The world is to me what Julia was to Saint Valentine,
And what the impoverished were to Nicholas Santa.
A world anemic in love needs a day to celebrate love,
I am a lover eternal, for me every day is valentine's day.
The world is my valentine, as such it is under my care,
It's my duty to protect it from Claudius' mischievous play.
I shall stop breathing before I break this pledge of mine.
There's no greater power than the pledge of a lover divine.

Sonnet 60

I ain't no idealist, but a biologist so,
I say, it's okay to want to be loved blind.
But if you can love despite coldness,
That is what makes you a lover divine.
Craving for affection will always be there,
Which is very much human in nature.
But you know what's more human than that,
The capacity to still love past such desire.
To love and to be loved is a great experience,
Greater still is to love without being loved.
True love's labor is a reward of its own,
Sheer sanctity is the sight of a lover on guard.
Where there is love unconditional, there is divinity.
Where there is condition, there is depravity.

Sonnet 61

What is humane is divine,
What is kind is holy.
What is humble is serene,
What is gentle is poetry.
Where there is conscience,
There is righteousness.
Where there is virtue,
There is godliness.
Practice humanity over doctrines,
Practice community over scriptures.
Doctrines have caused much division,
Because humans are sucker for dogmas.
Place all attention on behavior over belief.
Virtuous behavior brings social uplift.

22. Belief & Behavior (Sonnet 62 - 64)

Sonnet 62

Belief sustains a person,
But behavior sustains a society.
Belief has nothing to do with truth,
It is just a matter of mental necessity.
Often our belief defies all reason,
That's absolutely okay to a great extent.
What's not okay is to impose it on others,
To sentence others to our imprisonment.
I believe, that my teacher watches over me,
Even though he walks the earth no more.
This belief has nothing to do with your life,
But it helps me walk past my crippling woe.
All beliefs are good beliefs with or without reason,
If they help you in life to become a better person.

Sonnet 63

The time is always right to be kind,
The time is always right to lift a life.
The time is always right to refute hate,
The time is always right to conquer strife.
When the time is right, the right person,
Can change the world with the right cause.
The right time is this very moment,
And the right person is, you, who else!
Each of us are to be the home to another,
Each of us are to be the guard to another.
Whenever darkness shrouds another,
Each of us must rise as the lightbringer.
The time is always right to do what's right,
If not, then time is but a futile construct alright.

Sonnet 64

There is no time if the mind doesn't create it,
There is no reality if the mind doesn't create it.
There is no good if the mind doesn't create it,
There is no evil is the mind doesn't define it.
What we call evil is nature's necessity,
What we call good is nature's variation.
If we practice the good long enough,
It'll become our conviction and absolution.
Let's build our own time, let's build our own reality,
One that is founded on kindness, not cruelty.
Let's show Mother Nature we're unlike all her children,
Despite savagery within, we ain't bound to it as destiny.
DNA is destiny, so is mutation, hence no cruelty is permanent.
Civilization needs no magical intervention, just mortal commitment.

23. Poetry & Dawn (Sonnet 65 - 67)

Sonnet 65

If you wanna write – write.
If you wanna paint – paint.
If you wanna sing – sing.
If you wanna science – science.
If you wanna fly – fly.
If you wanna invent – invent.
If you wanna run for office – run.
If you wanna protect – protect.
If you wanna teach – teach.
If you wanna play – play.
If you wanna cook – cook.
If you wanna train – train.
Whatever you do, do with humanity,
And you'll set in motion a new reality.

Sonnet 66

Sonnet of Poetry

Poet is no servant of the dictionary,
Dictionary is servant to the poet.
Poet is no servant of language,
Language is servant to the poet.
It's poetry that makes the language,
Language makes no poetry, my friend.
Poet exists not to serve a linguist's whim,
But to breathe life into human language.
I've said repeatedly, language has limitations,
Only with poetry we can surpass some of 'em.
Sticklers for grammar make lousy poets,
If feeling doesn't surpass grammar, poetry it ain't.
Poetry is the most potent of all literary forms.
If prose is candle light, poetry is dawn.

Sonnet 67

I got tired of waiting for there to be dawn,
So I opened my eyes and became the dawn.
I got tired of waiting for there to be saneness,
So I stood and became saneness fully honed.
I got tired of waiting for there to be inclusion,
So I stood up as the epitome of inclusion.
I got tired of waiting for there to be ascension,
So I stood up as the example of ascension.
I got tired of waiting for there to be humility,
So I stood up and became humility incarnate.
I got tired of waiting for there to be gentleness,
So I rose as the maker of giants with gentleness.
I got tired of waiting for there to be undivision,
So I stood up as the definition of undivision.

24. The Humanitarian Fire
(Sonnet 68 - 70)

Sonnet 68

Undivided and uncorrupted,
That's the only way forward.
To treat all division in the world,
All you gotta do is disregard.
Regard neither sect of any kind,
Nor any of those ideologies.
If you gotta regard something,
Muster regard for human frailty.
Neither sectarian nor intellectual,
Heed no division of any form.
Heed only the sufferings of society,
'N all division will wither on their own.
Divisions don't disappear through policy,
But through individual acts of collectivity.

Sonnet 69

There is no sight sweeter than the sight of a person,
Acting genuinely in the best interest of the collective.
There is no sight uglier than the sight of an individual,
Yelling for reckless liberty while harming the collective.
There's no lasting way to ensure societal security,
Except putting oneself in harm's way for the collective.
There's no better way to sustain insecurity than,
To advocate sectarian security separate from collective.
History of animal kind is the history of self-preservation,
History of humankind is the history of self-sacrifice.
You gotta choose which history will you be a part of,
The history of humankind or history of the selfish kind?
Anything selfish is ugly, anything unselfish is sheer beauty.
Beauty lies in kinship of heart, not skinship of body.

Sonnet 70

I am on fire my friend,
And there's no putting it out.
You have only two choices,
Burn with me or run along now.
Humanitarian fire is unputoutable,
It can't be put out only passed along.
The question ain't who'll put me out,
But who's mad enough to burn along.
Little do the sober know this madness,
To them playing safe is the life's way.
But reformers ain't born to play safe,
We are born to gamble our life away.
The fire of oneness is a fire eternal.
The vessel changes, not the potential.

25. Lion in Sheep's Skin
(Sonnet 71 - 73)

Sonnet 71

Potential is universal,
Only difference is in intention.
Potential combined with intention,
Is the formula for epoch-making revolution.
No human is incapable of changing the world,
But most are unwilling to take responsibility.
Fundamental problem of this world ain't of law,
The fundamental problem of this world is apathy.
Everybody says that change begins with the self,
But how does it all begin in everyday ordinary life!
It begins when you turn from selfish to selfless,
When you expand and become the universal life.
So why worry my friend, whether you have potential!
The zillion dollar question is, is your zeal unshakable?

Sonnet 72

Close your eyes and take a leap of faith, o brave one,
Not in any outside magic but the one of your heart.
Have faith in the potential bestowed by mother nature,
And zealously march ahead as your dream's vanguard.
You are the dream, the dreamer, as well as its keeper,
Never give up, no matter the pangs of disappointment.
Dream lives so long as we work for it despite difficulty,
Step up, and half the dream is realized, despite torment.
It's more about perseverance than it's about patience,
Only those with shaky zeal are lost in patience's tale.
Those on a mission have no time to prove anything,
They are far too busy making the impossible possible.
With zeal unshakable we shall climb the hill unclimbable.
It's your climb, you gotta decide the outcome, not sheeple.

Sonnet 73

Better a lion in sheep's skin,
Than a sheep in lion's skin.
Better a giant in a gentle vessel,
Than germs in a fancy canteen.
When not needed act mostly a sheep,
But occasionally you gotta let the lion out.
Be a disinfectant and sanitize the world,
Not germs that make disease break out.
All social sickness is caused by selfishness,
And hypocrisy is what makes things worse.
Wipe out all hypocrisy from your being's core,
The world is a reflection of what's in our heart.
I say again, lion on the inside, sheep on the out.
When chihuahuas wreak havoc, let the dinosaur out.

26. All Messed Up (Sonnet 74 - 76)

Sonnet 74

Be the clown to those who cry,
Be the joker to those who joke.
Be an elephant to the intellectuals,
Be a dinosaur to those who croak.
But first hone your powers, bud,
Your powers of observation.
Learn to observe without judgment,
Observe people and their condition.
Not all rough exteriors are same inside,
Not all sweet exteriors are same inside.
Things are rarely ever black and white,
Be aware of the grey areas of society 'n life.
When you are born with awareness anew,
The whole world will find a home in you.

Sonnet 75

Let me hold your hand,
Let me be your home.
Here, take my heart,
Heart to heart life is honed.
There is no I, only Us,
There is no Us, only I.
Sounds confusing, right!
Because Love is across all Us and I.
In love all of me is you,
In love all of you is me.
In love it's all messed up,
The sweetest mess we could ever be.
So come, let's be messed up together.
Perhaps then things might get a little clear.

Sonnet 76

A beautiful mind creates a beautiful kind,
A beautiful kind creates a beautiful tide,
A beautiful tide creates a beautiful sight,
A beautiful sight creates a beautiful light,
A beautiful light creates a beautiful might,
A beautiful might creates a beautiful hide,
A beautiful hide creates a beautiful height,
A beautiful height creates a beautiful glide,
A beautiful glide creates a beautiful time,
A beautiful time creates a beautiful hind,
A beautiful hind creates a beautiful grind,
A beautiful grind creates a beautiful kite,
A beautiful kite creates a beautiful flight,
A beautiful flight creates a beautiful life.

27. To End Up Together
(Sonnet 77 - 79)

Sonnet 77

Be a muse to the world, not a mole.
Be a flute to the world, not a fluke.
Be a whistle to the world, not a hoax.
Be a warm coat to the world, not a coup.
Be O2 to the world, not CO.
Be water to the world, not booze.
Be a castle to the world, not another chaos.
Be ointment to the world, not another wound.
If you can't be a castle, be an apartment,
If you can't be an apartment, be a hut.
It's not about the size of your sacrifice,
It's about the intent, you impetuous lovenut!
Be a lamp, ladder or lego, what, it doesn't matter.
Just be something that makes the world better.

Sonnet 78

Two is better than one,
Seven billion is better than two.
It's okay to collide on occasion so long as,
We're by each other when we are in doo-doo.
Every time we hold hands, magic happens,
This ain't the magic of our ignorant ancestors.
I am talkin' about the mortal magic of diversity,
The power that comes to life when we're together.
Remember this simple principle my friend,
Those who fall together, fly together.
Arms are just arms when separated,
But shield when held together.
We are a blessing when we stand together.
When divided, we are our worst nightmare.

Sonnet 79

When we end up together,
That's not an end, but the beginning.
It's division that ends all journey,
End division, 'n life will have true beginning.
Century after century went on with division,
Yet unity is forever, division is nonexistence.
To breathe, eat, mate and sleep, ain't existence,
To help, heal, lift and light, that's existence.
We've got intellect, we've got sentiment,
All are useless if they don't help erase division.
Human is another name for undivision,
Not another synonym for discrimination.
To have 'n to hold, mustn't be a vow between just two.
Make it one among all, and soon unity will be true.

28. Simple & Ordinary (Sonnet 80 - 82)

Sonnet 80

By being ordinary we get to be extraordinary.
By being simple, we get to be spectacular.
By being an outspoken idiot, we rise as sage.
By being humble, we become truth's hammer.
By being gentle, we get to be giants.
By being magnanimous, we rise magnificent.
By being a servant, we get to be the leader.
By being annihilated, we rise as omnipresent.
By being self-regulated, we need less regulation.
By being accountable, we need less law and policy.
By denouncing supremacy, we start treating bigotry.
By rejecting exclusivity, we put an end to disparity.
There's no all-seeing eye, there's no all-knowing heart.
But if you see suffering and know to help, that's enough.

Sonnet 81

Sometimes I'm Gringo,
Sometimes I'm Turkish,
Sometimes I'm Latino,
Sometimes I'm Nordic.
Sometimes I'm british,
Sometimes I'm Balkan,
Sometimes I'm scientist.
Sometimes theologian.
Sometimes I'm dervish,
Sometimes I'm humanist,
Sometimes bodhisattva,
Sometimes nondualist.
Above all these labels be sure of one thing,
All the time, every time, I am a human being.

Sonnet 82

More ungroomed the artist,
More spectacular the art.
More ungroomed the writer,
More powerful the literature.
More ungroomed the scientist,
More impact their science makes.
More ungroomed the philosopher,
More impact their insight makes.
More ungroomed the poet,
More profound the poetry.
A reformer is always ungroomed,
Only then they make a beautiful society.
Grooming often implies a shallow interior.
Simpler the appearance, stronger the character.

29. Grooming & Dust Cleaning
(Sonnet 83 - 85)

Sonnet 83

Grooming is not a bad thing but,
It mustn't be placed above character.
Use grooming as an aid to life,
Never as life's ultimate desire.
If grooming makes you feel confident,
By all means, groom however you like.
Just remember, it's a slippery slope,
Grooming has a tendency to take over life.
The purpose of a car is not to buy gas,
Purpose of a car is to reach a destination.
The purpose of a life is not grooming,
Purpose of a life is to realize an ambition.
It's more important to know why than how to groom.
All the grooming in the world can't make a heart bloom.

Sonnet 84

All the grooming in the world,
Cannot make humanity bloom.
You can dress up a chimp in a fancy suit,
It doesn't clean their upstairs room.
Everybody spring cleans their home religiously,
They want their surroundings to be all tidy.
Yet they care diddly-squat about the chronic dust,
Gathering in their mind century after century.
Clean mind creates clean society,
And we ain't gonna achieve it with policy.
How you behave when nobody is watching,
That is the actual, genuine nature of society.
We gotta build character beyond outfit and policy.
Let's move from a synthetic society to one of integrity.

Sonnet 85

Enough with leaving this world,
In the hands of old fuddy-duddies.
Mark you, I ain't talkin' about age,
I am talkin' about mental maturity.
Long enough we've allowed tradition,
To wreak havoc on our precious planet.
It's time for reason and nonrigidity,
To stand up and take charge, all unbent.
Inhumanity persists in our world,
Because the humans give a consensual wave.
It's time for the grown-ups to grow up and,
Redeem reins from those with both feet in the grave.
Ancient relics belong in museum, not in driver's seat.
It's for the young ot head 'n heart to get the society lit.

30. Soulmate (Sonnet 86 - 88)

Sonnet 86

Be a soulmate to society 'n protect it,
From its past as well as the future.
Whence will come this society's ascension,
If it doesn't come from your unselfish desire.
Bite the dust again and again, it's okay,
There's nothing undignified in biting dust.
But know that no dust can keep you in dust,
Until you accept your setback as permanent.
All this world needs is just one human,
One human who won't brush off their duty,
The duty to act as a living, breathing human,
The duty to act as a pillar of undefiable dignity.
The world needs a safe haven, o soldier of love 'n truth.
It ain't gonna come from no church, no capitol, but you.

Sonnet 87

Be the melody in the heart of humanity,
Be the delight in the sight of humanity.
Be the comity in the spine of humanity,
Be the motion in the head of humanity.
To rearrange the world we gotta start,
With rearranging our priorities.
Start with changing your priority,
Before you go about changing policies.
Make your life the most awe-inspiring days,
Of human history, since the beginning.
Live as the person that has never lived,
And death will be just a flicker on your shimmering.
To lead the way for the next generation of humanity,
We gotta better ourselves across our ancestors' stupidity.

Sonnet 88

The Parenting Sonnet

Anybody can make a baby, that's no glory,
To raise a true being, that's a glorious thing.
It takes less than a minute to make a baby,
But more than a decade to make a being.
So if you choose to have baby someday,
Focus on their character, not just sustenance.
And make sure to keep luxury away from them,
For luxury is curse for character development.
Pass on the tradition of compassion to them,
Be a living example of the possibility of humanity.
Teach them the belief of nondiscrimination,
Demonstrate to them a never-before seen sanity.
Be the person you want the kids to grow up to be.
The best kind of parenting is that of exemplarity.

31. Be Unobvious (Sonnet 89 - 91)

Sonnet 89

Where would the world be,
Without its examples!
Where would the world be,
Without its amiables!
Where would the world be,
Without its pillars!
Where would the world be,
Without its builders!
Where would the world be,
Without its meddlers!
Where would the world be,
Without its caretakers!
Let me tell you where - exactly where it's today,
So, Arise O Caretakers, the mission awaits!

Sonnet 90

Tyrants are plenty, servants are scarce,
It ain't about leading, it's about service.
A moment of servanthood is worth,
More than a lifetime of leadership.
Be the last first human standing,
Do what's needed to restrain the retards.
And nature will raise up an army,
Of first humans to stand as vanguards.
Before the world possesses you,
With its snobbish and materialistic tenets,
Manifest your absurd sense of servanthood,
And possess the world against all selfish elements.
If you wanna lose control, lose control in sacrifice.
And you'll end up the very insignia of a good life.

Sonnet 91

Every life is obvious,
For every life is born selfish.
You for one be the unobvious,
Be the line between human 'n rubbish.
Once you are dead and gone,
What will be left of you!
Not the fortune you hoard,
But only the memories caused by you.
Whether or not you wake up the next day,
Go to bed knowing, you've lived as human.
Spend just one day as a human, and you'll cause,
More lasting reform than a decade of legal action.
Reform doesn't come from legal maneuverability,
But an unsubmissive yet accountable citizenry.

32. Citizen Lover (Sonnet 92 - 94)

Sonnet 92

There is no love without sacrifice,
There is no sacrifice without love.
In genuine love you wanna give all,
In genuine love there is no reserve.
Love my friend, love each and love all,
Love is the only language known to all.
When love becomes your first nature,
All personal pleasure feels dismal.
Wellbeing of the other is wellbeing of mine,
Thus feels the actual lover genuine.
Blessed are they who feel longing for people,
Such longing is the elixir to all that is sickening.
When such fire of love courses through our veins,
No reform on planet earth will remain unattained.

Sonnet 93

Citizen Lover
(The Sonnet)

Citizen lover is citizen justice,
All others are citizens of malice.
Love begets justice, whereas,
Judgment produces more malice.
All think, justice is an independent force,
But, justice is simply a descendant of love.
Where there is love, justice prevails,
Otherwise, there's just talk of justice 'n love.
Pledge allegiance to no judgment by intellect,
But only to love and love alone, my friend.
Where there is a place for love,
There is place for everything else.
Once a person has realized love untaintable,
They've achieved everything celebratable.

Sonnet 94

How will you know you've realized love?
When people no longer appear at a distance.
When they no longer appear as people,
But as reflection of your own essence.
When the other becomes I,
I becomes universal.
In that universal I all that there is,
Is an echo of the people.
The I is in all people,
But people are not in all the I.
That is why we suffer so much,
That is why we all cry, cry and cry.
If one dies thinking of people,
They will live on through people.

33. The Reflection (Sonnet 95 - 97)

Sonnet 95

If your knowledge of all the books,
Doesn't bring you closer to people,
Then what's the point of it all,
What's the point of being intellectually able!
If knowledge doesn't make you kind,
It is no knowledge, only a stubborn illusion.
If knowledge doesn't make you undivided,
It is no knowledge, only degradation.
First and foremost purpose of knowledge,
Is to erase the divide amongst people.
Yet today we use it to attain comfort,
Such is no human endeavor, but that of vegetable.
Only they are learned who learn to bring reformation.
All others fly blind in the eternal pit of argumentation.

Sonnet 96

Only a few understand the language of intellect,
Then most of them arrogantly boast and trod.
But from the tallest mountain to tiniest grass,
Everyone understands the language of love.
I've practiced all faith 'n ideology for a brief period,
And I accept all of them to be equally human.
That is why everyone thinks of me as their very own,
Everyone thinks, I am their own school's person.
I have no sect of my own, yet I am in every sect,
I have no school of my own, yet I am in every school.
One who loves, loves all no matter their label,
And finds a reflection in all beings including the fool.
There is no two, but only One that there ever is.
All separation is the sign of a spirit selfish.

Sonnet 97

One who knows the self,
Finds the self in everyone.
One who know home,
Finds home in everyone.
One who has love,
Finds love in everyone.
One who has goodness,
Finds goodness in everyone.
One who has potential,
Finds potential in everyone.
One who knows life,
Finds life in everyone.
One only finds outside what's inside.
Society is a reflection of a human upright.

34. The Highest Meditation
(Sonnet 98 – 100)

Sonnet 98

Only human is the doer,
All others are destroyer.
Only savages live on pedestal,
A human toils in the soil as reformer.
Water never stands still on a pedestal,
It always flows down to the lowest ground.
Be a stream of gentle water and boldly rush,
To those forgotten by the fools who frown.
Be the breeze, be the water,
Be the serene shade of a heartful tree.
In character be an elephant,
Gentle, unafraid and forever free.
Free are they who have no walls inside,
All others are prisoners of their own divisionist pride.

Sonnet 99

Servant-consciousness is God-consciousness,
All else is animal-consciousness.
Lover-consciousness is God-consciousness,
All else is animal-consciousness.
To serve the helpless is to help oneself,
To make another smile is to realize life.
Service and service alone is life,
Whereas everything else is death in disguise.
Service alone is the path of civilization,
All else is path of the stoneage.
Cherish the path of service and sacrifice,
No other path holds a candle to its exuberance.
All meditate on a chant or a symbol,
The highest meditation is the meditation on people.

Sonnet 100

All meditate on symbols,
I meditate on people.
Most worship fictitious deities,
I worship those branded unliftable.
People are my almighty,
Oneness is my religion,
Division is degradation,
Unification is illumination.
All is possible for a human who's responsible,
Only the indifferent make excuses.
Possibility is born of responsibility,
Not of whining, praying and limbless wishes.
Real and unreal, put all these talk aside.
Let us be civilization, let us be lifelight.

BIBLIOGRAPHY

Archer M., (2000), Being Human: The Problem of Agency. Cambridge University Press.

Adolphs R (2003) Cognitive neuroscience of human social behaviour. Nature Rev Neurosci 4: 165–178.

Adolphs R, Tranel D, Damasio AR (2003) Dissociable neural systems for recognizing emotions. Brain Cogn 52: 61–69.

Andresen, Jensine, and Robert Forman, eds. Cognitive Models and Spiritual Maps. Bowling Green, Ohio: Imprint Academic, 2000.

Azari, Nina, Janpeter Nickel, Gilbert Wunderlich, Michael Niedeggen, Harald Hefter, Lutz Tellmann, Hans Herzog, Petra Stoerig, Dieter Birnbacher, and Rudiger Seitz. "Neural

Correlates of Religious Experience." European Journal of Neuroscience 13, no. 8 (2001)

Agar, N. (2004). Liberal eugenics: In defence of human enhancement. London: Blackwell Publishing.

Alteheld, N., Roessler, G., Vobig, M., & Walter, R. (2004). The retina implant new approach to a visual prosthesis. Biomedizinische Technik, 49(4), 99–103.

Antal, A., Nitsche, M. A., Kincses, T. Z., Kruse, W., Hoffmann, K. P., & Paulus, W. (2004a). Facilitation of visuo-motor learning by transcranial direct current stimulation of the motor and extrastriate visual areas in humans. European Journal of Neuroscience, 19(10), 2888–2892.

Bernstein R.J., (1971), Praxis and Action: Contemporary Philosophies of Human Activity. Philadelphia: University of Pennsylvania Press.

Bernstein R.J., (1976), The Restructuring Social and Political Thought.

Bernstein R.J., (1983), Beyond Relativism and Objectivism: Science, Hermeneutics, and Praxis. Philadelphia: University of Pennsylvania Press.

Bernstein R.J., (1986), Philosophical Profiles. Philadelphia: University of Pennsylvania Press.

Bernstein R.J., (1991), New Constellation. Cambridge: MIT Press.

Birkhead, T. R., Johnson, S. D. & Nettleship, D. N. (1985). Extra-pair matings and mate guarding in the common murre Uria aalge. - Anim. Behav. 33, p. 608-619.

Beauregard, Mario, and Vincent Paquette. "Neural Correlates of a Mystical Experience in Carmelite Nuns." Neuroscience Letters 405, no. 3 (2006)

Benson, Herbert. Timeless Healing: The Power and Biology of Belief. New York: Scribner, 1996

Bose, Subhas Chandra. An Indian Pilgrim: An Unfinished Autobiography, Oxford University Press, 1997

Bogen, J.E.(1995a), 'On the neurophysiology of consciousness: Part I. An overview', Consciousness and Cognition, 4.

Bogen, J.E. (1995b), 'On the neurophysiology of consciousness: Part II. Constraining the semantic problem', Consciousness and Cognition, 4.

Bremner, J. D., R. Soufer, et al. (2001). "Gender differences in cognitive and neural correlates of remembrance of emotional words." Psychopharmacol Bull 35 (3).

Brothers, L. (2002). The social brain: A project for integrating primate behavior and neurophysiology in a new domain. In J. T. Cacioppo et al. (Eds.), Foundations in neuroscience. Cambridge, MA: MIT Press.

Buss, D. D. (2003). Evolutionary Psychology: The New Science of Mind, 2nd ed. New York: Allyn & Bacon.

Buss, D. M. (1989). "Conflict between the sexes: Strategic interference and the evocation of anger and upset." J Pers Soc Psychol 56 (5).

Buss, D. M. (1995). "Psychological sex differences. Origins through sexual selection." Am Psychol 50 (3).

Buss, D. M., and D. P. Schmitt (1993). "Sexual strategies theory: An evolutionary perspective on human mating." Psychol Rev 100 (2).

Blakemore SJ, Decety J (2001) From the perception of action to the understanding of intention. Nature Rev Neurosci 2: 561.

Colapietro V., (1988), "Human Agency: The Habits of Our Being." Southern Journal of Philosophy, XXVI, 2, pp. 153-68.

Colapietro V., (1992), "Purpose, Power, and Agency." The Monist, 75, 4 (October) pp. 423-44.

Colapietro V., (2004a), "C. S. Peirce's Reclamation of Teleology." Nature in American Philosophy, ed. Jean De Groot (Washington, D.C.: Catholic University Press of America), pp. 88-108.

Carey DP, Perrett DI, Oram MW (1997) Recognizing, understanding and reproducing actions. In: Jeannerod M, Grafman J (eds) Handbook of neuropsychology. Vol. 11: Action and cognition. Elsevier, Amsterdam.

Carr L, Iacoboni M, Dubeau MC, Mazziotta JC, Lenzi GL (2003) Neural mechanisms of empathy in humans: a relay from neural systems for imitation to limbic areas. Proc Natl Acad Sci USA 100: 5497–5502.

Chomsky Noam, (2017) Requiem for the American Dream

Chomsky Noam, (2016) Who Rules the World?

Chomsky Noam, (2010) How the World Works

Churchland, P.S. (1986), Neurophilosophy (Cambridge, MA: The MIT Press).

Churchland, P.S. & Ramachandran, V.S. (1993), 'Filling in: Why Dennett is wrong', in Dennett and His Critics: Demystifying Mind, ed. B. Dahlbom (Oxford: Blackwell Scientific Press).

Churchland, P.S., Ramachandran, V.S. & Sejnowski, T.J. (1994), 'A critique of pure vision', in Large- scale Neuronal Theories of the Brain, ed. C. Koch & J.L. Davis (Cambridge, MA: The MIT Press).

Coyle EF. Integration of the physiological factors determining endurance performance ability. Exerc Sport Sci Rev. 1995;23:25–63.

Crick, F. (1994), The Astonishing Hypothesis: The Scientific Search for the Soul (New York: Simon and Schuster).

Crick, F. (1996), 'Visual perception: rivalry and consciousness', Nature, 379.

Crick, F. & Koch, C. (1992), 'The problem of consciousness', Scientific American, 267.

Damasio, A (2003a) Looking for Spinoza. Harcourt Inc. Damasio A (2003b) Feeling of emotion and the self. Ann NY Acad Sci 1001: 253–261.

d'Aquili, Eugene. "Senses of Reality in Science and Religion." Zygon 17, no 4 (1982)

d'Aquili, Eugene. "The Biopsychological Determinants of Religious Ritual Behavior." Zygon 10, no. 1 (1975)

d'Aquili, Eugene. "The Myth-Ritual Complex: A Biogenetic Structural Analysis." Zygon 18, no. 3 (1983)

d'Aquili, Eugene, and Andrew Newberg. The Mystical Mind: Probing the Biology of Religious Experience. Minneapolis: Fortress Press, 1999.

Daly DD. 1958. Ictal affect. Am J Psychiatry.

Damasio, A. (1994) Descartes' Error: Emotion, Reason and the Human Brain. New York, Putnams.

Damasio, A. (1999) The Feeling of What Happens: Body, Emotion and the Making of Consciousness. London, Heinemann.

Darwin, C. (1859) On the Origin of Species by Means of Natural Selection. London, Murray.

Darwin, C. (1871) The Descent of Man and Selection in Relation to Sex. London, John Murray.

Darwin, C. (1872) The Expression of the Emotions in Man and Animals. London, John Murray; also published 1965, Chicago, University of Chicago Press.

Dawkins, M.S. (1987) Minding and mattering. In C. Blakemore and S. Greenfield (eds) Mindwaves. Oxford, Blackwell, 151-60.

Dawkins, R. (1976) The Selfish Gene. Oxford, Oxford University Press; a new edition, with additional material, was published in 1989.

Di Pellegrino G, Fadiga L, Fogassi L, Gallese V, Rizzolatti G (1992) Understanding motor events: A neurophysiological study. Exp Brain Res 91: 176–80.

Deikman, A.J. (2000) A functional approach to mysticism. Journal of Consciousness Studies 7(11-12), 75-91.

Delmonte, M.M. (1987) Personality and meditation. In M. West (ed.) The Psychology of Meditation. Oxford, Clarendon Press, 118-32.

Dennett, D.C. (1988) Quining qualia. In A.J. Marcel and E. Bisiach (eds) Consciousness in Contemporary Science. Oxford, Oxford University Press, 42-77.

Dennett, D.C. (1991) Consciousness Explained. Boston, MA, and London, Little, Brown and Co.

Dennett, D.C. (1995a) Darwin's Dangerous Idea. London, Penguin.

Dennett, D.C. (1998b) Brainchildren: Essays on Designing Minds. Cambridge, MA, MIT Press.

Dewhurst, Kenneth, and A. W. Beard. "Sudden Religious Conversions in Temporal Lobe Epilepsy." British Journal of Psychiatry 117 (1970)

Dewhurst K, Beard AW. Sudden religious conversions in temporal lobe epilepsy. 1970 Epilepsy Behav 2003

Devinsky O, Lai G. Spirituality and religion in epilepsy. Epilepsy Behav 2008.

Devinsky, O., Morrell, MJ, Vogt, BA. (1995) 'Contribution of anterior cingulate cortex to behavior', Brain, 118.

E. Horvitz, "One Hundred Year Study on Artificial Intelligence: Reflections and Framing," ed: Stanford University, 2014.

Eckhart Meister, Selected Writings

Egidi R., ed. (1999), "Von Wright and 'Dante's Dream': Stages in a Philosophical Pilgrim's Progress", in

In Search of a New Humanism: the Philosophy of G.H. von Wright, ed. by R. Egidi, Kluwer, Dordrecht.

Fadiga L, Fogassi L, Pavesi G, Rizzolatti G (1995) Motor facilitation during action observation: a magnetic stimulation study. J Neurophysiol 73: 2608–2611.

Fogassi L, Gallese V, Fadiga L, Rizzolatti G (1998) Neurons responding to the sight of goal directed hand/arm actions in the parietal area PF (7b) of the macaque monkey. Soc Neurosci Abs 24:257.5.

Frith U, Frith CD (2003) Development and neurophysiology of mentalizing. Philos Trans R Soc Lond B Biol Sci 358: 459.

Farah, M.J. (1989), 'The neural basis of mental imagery', Trends in Neurosciences, 10.

Finlay BL, Darlington RB (1995) Linked regularities in the development and evolution of mammalian brains. Science 268.

Freud, S. "The Interpretation of Dreams", 1900

Freud, S. "Selected papers on hysteria and other psychoneuroses" Journal of Nervous and Mental Disease 1909.

Freud, S. "The Origin and Development of Psychoanalysis", 1910

Freud, S. "Psychopathology of everyday life", 1914

Freud, S. "Beyond the Pleasure Principle", 1920

Frith, C.D. & Dolan, R.J. (1997), 'Abnormal beliefs: Delusions and memory', Paper presented at the May, 1997, Harvard Conference on Memory and Belief.

Gay, Volney, ed. Neuroscience and Religion. Plymouth, UK: Lexington Books, 2009.

Gazzaniga, M. S. (1985). The social brain. New York: Basic Books.

Gazzaniga, M.S. (1993), 'Brain mechanisms and conscious experience', Ciba Foundation Symposium, 174.

Geschwind N. "Behavioural changes in temporal lobe epilepsy". Psychol Med. 1979.

Gellhorn, E., Kiely, W.F. "Mystical states of consciousness: neurophysiological and clinical aspects." J Nerv Ment Dis. 1972;154:399-405.

Gilbert SL, Dobyns WB, Lahn BT (2005) Genetic links between brain development and brain evolution. Nat Rev Genet 6.

Gray JA. The Psychology of Fear and Stress. 2nd ed. New York, NY: Cambridge University Press; 1988.

Gloor, P. (1992), 'Amygdala and temporal lobe epilepsy', in The Amygdala: Neurobiological Aspects of Emotion, Memory and Mental Dysfunction, ed J.P. Aggleton (New York: Wiley-Liss).

Greenspan, S. I. and S. G. Shanker (2004). The first idea: How symbols, language, and intelligence evolved from our early primate ancestors to modern humans. Cambridge, MA: Da Capo Press.

Grady, D. (1993), 'The vision thing: Mainly in the brain', Discover, June.

Gallagher HL, Frith CD (2003) Functional imaging of 'theory of mind'. Trends Cogn Sci 7: 77.

Gallese V, Fogassi L, Fadiga L, Rizzolatti G (2002) Action representation and the inferior parietal lobule. In: Prinz W, Hommel B (eds) Attention & Performance XIX. Common mechanisms in perception and action. Oxford University Press, Oxford.

Gallese V, Keysers C, Rizzolatti G (2004) A unifying view of the basis of social cognition. Trends Cogn Sci 8: 396–403.

Goldman AI, Sripada CS (2004) Simulationist models of face-based emotion recognition. Cognition 94: 193–213.

Grèzes J, Costes N, Decety J (1998) Top-down effect of strategy on the perception of human biological motion: a PET investigation. Cogn Neuropsychol 15: 553–582.

Grèzes J, Armony JL, Rowe J, Passingham RE (2003) Activations related to "mirror" and "canonical" neurones in the human brain: an fMRI study. Neuroimage 18: 928–937.

Gross CG, Rocha-Miranda CE, Bender DB (1972) Visual properties of neurons in the inferotemporal cortex of the macaque. J Neurophysiol 35: 96–111.

Guevara Che, The Motorcycle Diaries, 1992

Hari R, Forss N, Avikainen S, Kirveskari S, Salenius S, Rizzolatti G (1998) Activation of human primary motor cortex during action observation: a neuromagnetic study. Proc. Natl Acad Sci USA 95: 15061–15065.

Hardy, G. H. (1940). Ramanujan. Cambridge: Cambridge University Press.

Hall, Daniel, Keith Meador, and Harold Koenig. "Measuring Religiousness in Health Research: Review and Critique." Journal of Religion and Health 47, no. 2 (2008)

Harris, Sam, Jonas Kaplan, Ashley Curiel, Susan Bookheimer, Marco Iacoboni, and Mark Cohen. "The Neural Correlates of Religious and

Nonreligious Belief." PLoS One 4, no. 10 (October 1, 2009)

Halgren, E. (1992), 'Emotional neurophysiology of the amygdala within the context of human cognition', in The Amygdala: Neurobiological Aspects of Emotion, Memory and Mental Dysfunction, ed J.P. Aggleton (New York: Wiley-Liss).

Halligan PW, Fink GR, Marshal JC, Vallar G. 2003. Spatial cognition: evidence from visual neglect. Trends Cogn Sci.

Handbook of Emotions, Edited by Michael Lewis, Jeannette M. Haviland-Jones, and Lisa Feldman Barrett, The Guilford Press; 3rd edition (2010).

Hameroff, S.R. and Penrose, R. (1996) Conscious events as orchestrated space-time selections. Journal of Consciousness Studies 3(1), 36-53; also reprinted in J. Shear (ed.) (1997) Explaining Consciousness-The Hard

Problem. Cambridge, MA, MIT Press, 177-95.

Harding, D.E. (1961) On Having no Head: Zen and the Re-Discovery of the Obvious. London, Buddhist Society.

Hardy, A. (1979) The Spiritual Nature of Man: A Study of Contemporary Religious Experience. Oxford, Clarendon Press.

Harre, R. and Gillett, G. (1994) The Discursive Mind. Thousand Oaks, CA, Sage.

Haugeland, J. (ed.) (1997) Mind Design II: Philosophy, Psychology, Artificial Intelligence. Cambridge, MA, MIT Press.

Hauser, M.D. (2000) Wild Minds: What Animals Really Think. New York, Henry Holt and Co.; London, Penguin.

Hebb, D.O. (1949) The Organization of Behavior. New York, Wiley.

Helmholtz, H.L.F. von (1856-67) Treatise on Physiological Optics.

Hess, EH (1975) "The role of pupil size in communication," Scientific American, 233(5), 110–12.

Heyes, C.M. (1998) Theory of mind in nonhuman primates. Behavioral and Brain Sciences 21, 101-48; with commentaries.

Heyes, C.M. and Galef, B.G. (eds) (1996) Social Learning in Animals: The Roots of Culture. San Diego, CA, Academic Press.

Hilgard, E.R. (1986) Divided Consciousness: Multiple Controls in Human Thought and Action. New York, Wiley.

Hilton, E.N., Lundberg, T.R. Transgender Women in the Female Category of Sport: Perspectives on Testosterone Suppression and Performance Advantage. Sports Med 51, 199–214 (2021).

Hitler, Adolf. Mein Kampf, 1925

Hodgson, R. (1891) A case of double consciousness. Proceedings of the Society for Psychical Research 7, 221-58.

Hofstadter, D.R. and Dennett, D.C. (eds) (1981) The Mind's I: Fantasies and Reflections on Self and Soul. London, Penguin.

Holland, J. (ed.) (2001) Ecstasy: The Complete Guide: A Comprehensive Look at the Risks and Benefits of MDMA. Rochester, VT, Park Street Press.

Holmes, D.S. (1987) The influence of meditation versus rest on physiological arousal. In M. West (ed.) The Psychology of Meditation. Oxford, Clarendon Press, 81-103.

Holmstrom, David. 1992, Christian Science Monitor

Holt, J. (1999) Blindsight in debates about qualia. Journal of Consciousness Studies 6(5), 54-71.

Holloway RL (1996) Evolution of the human brain. In: Lock A, Peters CR (eds) Handbook of human symbolic evolution. Oxford University Press, Oxford

Iacoboni M, Woods RP, Brass M, Bekkering H, Mazziotta JC, Rizzolatti G (1999) Cortical mechanisms of human imitation. Science 286: 2526–2528.

Iacoboni M, Koski LM, Brass M, Bekkering H, Woods RP, Dubeau MC, Mazziotta JC, Rizzolatti G (2001) Reafferent copies of imitated actions in the right superior temporal cortex. Proc Natl Acad Sci USA 98: 13995–13999.

Jeannerod M (1988) The neural and behavioural organization of goal-directed movements. Clarendon Press, Oxford.

Johnson-Frey SH, Maloof FR, Newman-Norlund R, Farrer C, Inati S, Grafton ST (2003) Actions or hand-objects interactions? Human inferior frontal cortex and action observation. Neuron 39: 1053–1058.

Jackson, F. (1982) Epiphenomenal qualia. Philosophical Quarterly 32, 127-36.

James, W. (1890) The Principles of Psychology (2 volumes). London, Macmillan.

James, W. (1902) The Varieties of Religious Experience: A Study in Human Nature. New York and London, Longmans, Green and Co.

Jansen, K. (2001) Ketamine: Dreams and Realities. Sarasota, FL, Multidisciplinary Association for Psychedelic Studies.

Jay, M. (ed.) (1999) Artificial Paradises: A Drugs Reader. London, Penguin.

Jaynes, J. (1976) The Origin of Consciousness in the Breakdown of the Bicameral Mind. New York, Houghton Mifflin.

Johnson, M.K. and Raye, C.L. (1981) Reality monitoring. Psychological Review 88, 67-85.

Kadim I, Mahgoub O, Baqir S et al. (2015) Cultured meat from muscle stem cells: a review of challenges and prospects. J Integr Agr 14: 222–233

Kandel, E. R. In Search of Memory: The Emergence of a New Science of Mind, W. W. Norton & Company (2007).

Kandel E. R. Schwartz JH, Jessel TM. Principles of neural sciences. New York; McGraw Hill, 2000.

Kanwisher, N. (2001) Neural events and perceptual awareness. Cognition

79, 89-113; also reprinted inS. Dehaene (ed.) The Cognitive Neuroscience of Consciousness. Cambridge, MA, MIT Press, 89-113.

Karn, K. and Hayhoe, M. (2000) Memory representations guide targeting eye movements in a natural task. Visual Cognition 7, 673-703.

Kennedy, H., & Dehay, C. (1988). Functional implications of the anatomical organization of the callosal projections of visual areas V1 and V2 in the macaque monkey. Behav. Brain Res., 29, 225–236.

Kentridge, R.W. and Heywood, C.A. (1999) The status of blindsight. Journal of Consciousness Studies 6(5), 3-11.

Kihlstrom, J.F. (1996) Perception without awareness of what is perceived, learning without awareness of what is learned. In M. Velmans (ed.) The Science of Consciousness. London, Routledge, 23-46.

Kosslyn, S.M. (1980) Image and Mind. Cambridge, MA, Harvard University Press.

Kosslyn, S.M. (1988) Aspects of a cognitive neuroscience of mental imagery. Science 240, 1621-6.

Kinsbourne, M. (1995), 'The intralaminar thalamic nucleii', Consciousness and Cognition, 4.

Kjaer, Troels, Camilla Bertelsen, Paola Piccini, David Brooks, Jorgen Alving, and Hans Lou. "Increased Dopamine Tone during Meditation- Induced Change of Consciousness." Cognitive Brain Research 13, no. 2 (April 2002)

Kölmel HW. 1985. Complex visual hallucinations in the hemianopic field. J Neurol Neurosurg Psychiatry.

Koenig, Harold. "Research on Religion, Spirituality, and Mental Health: A Review." Canadian Journal of Psychiatry 54, no. 5 (May 2009)

Koenig, Harold, ed. Handbook of Religion and Mental Health. San Diego, CA: Academic Press, 1998

Kraepelin E. Psychiatry: A Textbook for Students and Physicians. New York, NY: Science History Publications; 1990.

Lauglin, Charles, John McManus, and Eugene d'Aquili. Brain, Symbol, and Experience. 2nd ed. New York: Columbia University Press, 1992

Lakoff, G. and M. Johnson (1999). Philosophy in the flesh. Basic Books: New York.

LeDoux, J. E. (1996). The emotional brain. New York: Simon & Schuster.

LeDoux, J.E. (1992), 'Emotion and the amygdala', in The Amygdala: Neurobiological Aspects of Emo- tion, Memory and Mental Dysfunction, ed J.P. Aggleton (New York: Wiley-Liss).

Levin, D.T. and Simons, D.J. (1997) Failure to detect changes to attended objects in motion pictures. Psychonomic Bulletin and Review 4, 501-6.

Levine,J. (1983) Materialism and qualia: the explanatory gap. Pacific Philosophical Quarterly 64, 354-61.

Levine,J. (2001) Purple Haze: The Puzzle of Consciousness. New York, Oxford University Press. Levine, S. (1979) A Gradual Awakening. New York, Doubleday.

Lewicki, P., Czyzewska, M. and Hoffman, H. (1987) Unconscious acquisition of complex procedural knowledge. Journal of Experimental Psychology: Learning, Memory and Cognition 13, 523-30.

Lewicki, P., Hill, T. and Bizot, E. (1988) Acquisition of procedural knowledge about a pattern of stimuli that cannot be articulated. Cognitive Psychology 20, 24-37.

Lewicki, P., Hill, T. and Czyzewska, M. (1992) Nonconscious acquisition of information. American Psychologist 47, 796-801.

Mesulam MM, Mufson EJ (1982) Insula of the old world monkey. III: Efferent cortical output and comments on function. J Comp Neurol 212: 38–52.

Naskar, Abhijit. "Homo: A Brief History of Consciousness", 2015

Naskar, Abhijit. "What is Mind?", 2016

Naskar, Abhijit. "Love, God & Neurons: Memoir of A Scientist who found himself by getting lost", 2016

Naskar, Abhijit. "Principia Humanitas", 2017

Naskar, Abhijit. "We Are All Black: A Treatise on Racism", 2017

Naskar, Abhijit. "Either Civilized or Phobic: A Treatise on Homosexuality", 2017

Naskar, Abhijit. "The Bengal Tigress: A Treatise on Gender Equality", 2017

Naskar, Abhijit. "Morality Absolute", 2017

Naskar, Abhijit. "Build Bridges not Walls: In the name of Americana", 2018

Naskar, Abhijit. "Fabric of Humanity", 2018

Naskar, Abhijit. "Citizens of Peace: Beyond the Savagery of Sovereignty", 2019

Naskar, Abhijit. "The Constitution of The United Peoples of Earth", 2019

Naskar, Abhijit. "Neurons Giveth, Neurons Taketh Away | Abhijit Naskar | TEDxIIMRanchi", 2019 https://www.youtube.com/watch?v=BNX-Q0ySm80

Naskar, Abhijit. "Mission Reality", 2019

Naskar, Abhijit. "Operation Justice: To Make A Society That Needs No Law", 2019

Naskar, Abhijit. "Every Generation Needs Caretakers: The Gospel of Patriotism", 2020

Naskar, Abhijit. "Hurricane Humans: Give me accountability, I'll give you peace", 2020

Naskar, Abhijit. "Revolution Indomable", 2020

Naskar, Abhijit. "Servitude is Sanctitude", 2020

Naskar, Abhijit. "Good Scientist: When Science and Service Combine", 2020

Newberg, Andrew. "How God Changes Your Brain: An Introduction to Jewish Neurotheology", CCAR Journal: The Reform Jewish Quarterly, Winter 2016.

Newberg, Andrew, and Stephanie Newberg. "A Neuropsychological Perspective on Spiritual Development." In Handbook of Spiritual Development in Childhood and Adolescence, edited by Eugene Roehlkepartain, Pamela King, Linda Wagener, and Peter Benson. London: Sage Publications, Inc., 2005

Newberg, Andrew. "The Neurotheology Link An Intersection Between Spirituality and Health", Alternative and Complimentary Therapies, Vol 21 No 1, February 2015.

Newberg, Andrew, Nancy Wintering, Dharma Khalsa, Hannah Roggenkamp, and Mark Waldman. "Meditation Effects on Cognitive Function and Cerebral Blood Flow in Subjects with Memory Loss: A Preliminary Study." Journal of Alzheimer's Disease 20, no. 2 (2010)

Nash, M. (1995), 'Glimpses of the mind', Time.

Nesse RM. Proximate and evolutionary studies of anxiety, stress and depression: synergy at the interface. Neurosci Biobehav Rev. 1999;23:895-903.

Nicolelis, Miguel. (2011) "Beyond Boundaries: The New Neuroscience of Connecting Brains with Machines--- and How It Will Change Our Lives", Times Books

O'Hara, K. and Scutt, T. (1996) There is no hard problem of consciousness. Journal of Consciousness Studies 3(4), 290-302, reprinted in J. Shear (ed.) (1997) Explaining Consciousness. Cambridge, MA, MIT Press, 69-82.

O'Regan, J.K. (1992) Solving the "real" mysteries of visual perception: the world as an outside memory. Canadian Journal of Psychology 46, 461-88.

O'Regan, J.K. and Noe, A. (2001) A sensorimotor account of vision and visual consciousness. Behavioral and Brain Sciences 24(5), 883-917.

O'Regan, J.K., Rensink, R.A. and Clark,].]. (1999) Change-blindness as a result of "mudsplashes." Nature 398, 34.

Ornstein, R.E. (1977) The Psychology of Consciousness (2nd edn). New York, Harcourt.

Ornstein, R.E. (1986) The Psychology of Consciousness (3rd edn). New York, Pehguin.

Ornstein, R.E. (1992) The Evolution of Consciousness. New York, Touchstone.

Penfield W, Faulk ME (1955) The insula: further observations on its function. Brain 78: 445– 470.

Penrose, R. (1994), Shadows of the Mind (Oxford: Oxford University Press).

Penrose, R. (1989), The Emperor's New Mind: Concerning Computers, Minds and The Laws of Physics (Oxford: Oxford University Press).

Persinger, "'I would kill in God's name' role of sex, weekly church attendance, report of a religious experience and limbic lability" Perceptual and Motor Skills 1997.

Persinger "Experimental simulation of the God experience" Neurotheology 2003.

Persinger, Corradini, Clement, Keaney, et al "Neurotheology and its convergence with neuroquantology" NeuroQuantology 2010.

Persinger, Koren and St-Pierre "The electromagnetic induction of mystical and altered states within the laboratory" Journal of Consciousness Exploration and Research 2010.

Persinger "Case report: A prototypical spontaneous 'sensed presence' of a sentient being and concomitant electroencephalographic activity in the clinical laboratory" Neurocase 2008.

Persinger and Saroka "Potential production of Hughlings Jackson's "parasitic consciousness" by physiologically-patterned weak transcerebral magnetic fields: QEEG and source localization" Epilepsy & Behavior 28 (2013).

Persinger. "The neuropsychiatry of paranormal experiences". J Neuropsychiatry Clin Neurosci 2001.

Persinger. "Neuropsychological bases of god beliefs", New York: Praeger, 1987

Persinger. "Temporal lobe epileptic signs and correlative behaviors displayed by normal populations", Journal of General Psychology, 1986

Perry BD, Pollard R. Homeostasis, stress, trauma, and adaptation. A neurodevelopmental view of childhood trauma. Child Adolesc Psychiatr Clin N Am. 1998;7:33.

Puce A, Perrett D (2003) Electrophysiological and brain imaging of biological motion. Philosoph Trans Royal Soc Lond, Series B, 358: 435–445.

Ramachandran VS. Behavioral and magnetoencephalographic correlates of plasticity in the adult human brain. Proc Natl Acad Sci USA 1993; 90: 10413–20.

Ramachandran VS. Phantom limbs, neglect syndromes, repressed memories, and Freudian psychology. Int Rev Neurobiol 1994; 37: 291–333.

Ramachandran VS. Plasticity and functional recovery in neurology. Clin Med 2005; 5: 368–73.

Ramachandran VS, Hirstein W. The perception of phantom limbs. The D. O. Hebb lecture. Brain 1998; 121: 1603–30.

Ramachandran VS, Rogers-Ramachandran D, Cobb S. Touching the phantom limb. Nature 1995; 377: 489–90.

Ramachandran VS, Rogers-Ramachandran D. Phantom limbs and neural plasticity. Arch Neurol 2000; 57: 317–20.

Ramachandran VS, Rogers-Ramachandran D. It's all done with mirrors. Sci Am Mind 2007; 18: 16–9.

Ramachandran VS, Rogers-Ramachandran D. Sensations referred to a patient's phantom arm from another subjects intact arm: perceptual correlates of mirror neurons. Med Hypotheses 2008; 70: 1233–4.

Ramachandran VS, Rogers-Ramachandran D, Stewart M. Perceptual correlates of massive cortical reorganization. Science 1992; 258: 1159–60.

Rizzolatti G, Craighero L (2004) The mirror-neuron system. Annu Rev Neurosci 27: 169–192.

Rizzolatti G, Fogassi L, Gallese V (2001) Neurophysiological mechanisms underlying the understanding and imitation of action. Nature Rev Neurosci 2:661–670.

Rock I, Victor J. Vision and touch: an experimentally created conflict between the two senses. Science 1964; 143: 594–6.

Rose´n B, Lundborg G. Training with a mirror in rehabilitation of the hand. Scand J Plast Reconstr Surg Hand Surg 2005; 39: 104–8.

Roberts, TA; Smalley, J; Ahrendt, D (December 2020). "Effect of gender affirming hormones on athletic performance in transwomen and transmen: implications for sporting organisations and legislators". British

Journal of Sports Medicine. 55 (11): 577–583

Royet JP, Plailly J, Delon-Martin C, Kareken DA, Segebarth C (2003) fMRI of emotional responses to odors: influence of hedonic valence and judgment, handedness, and gender. Neuroimage 20: 713–728.

Rozin R Haidt J and McCauley CR (2000) Disgust. In: Lewis M, Haviland-Jones JM (eds) Handbook of Emotion. 2nd Edition. Guilford Press, New York, pp 637–653.

Saxe R, Carey S, Kanwisher N (2004) Understanding other minds: linking developmental psychology and functional neuroimaging. Annu Rev Psychol 55: 87–124.

S. J. Russell and P. Norvig, Artificial intelligence: a modern approach (3rd edition): Prentice Hall, 2009.

Smith A (1759) The theory of moral sentiments (ed. 1976). Clarendon Press, Oxford.

Schilling, Vincent. 2017, indian country today

Stein, Stephen K. 2017, The Sea in World History: Exploration, Travel, and Trade

Simonsen R (2015) Eating for the future: veganism and the challenge of in vitro meat. In: Stapleton P, Byers A (Hg). Biopolitics and utopia. Palgrave Macmillan, New York (2015), S 167–190

Tesla N. "My Inventions", 1919

T. R. Society, "Machine learning: the power and promise of computers that learn by example," ed. The Royal Society, 2017.

www.ingramcontent.com/pod-product-compliance
Lightning Source LLC
Chambersburg PA
CBHW051041250726
48656CB00001B/85